Sea, Land, Sky

A Dragon Magick Grimoire

Sea, Land, Sky

A Dragon Magick Grimoire

Parker J. Torrence

Three Moons Media

Copyright © 2002 Parker J. Torrence

All rights reserved. No part of this book may be reproduced or transmitted in any form or by any means, electronic or mechanical, including Internet usage, photocopying, recording or by any information storage and retrieval system, except for brief quotations embodied in critical articles and reviews, without permission in writing from the author.

Cover art by Wendy "Wolfrose" Torrence

Interior illustrations by Ashley "Moondancer" Bloss

Decorative fonts used on cover and some graphics:
Bard, by Corel Corp.
Zombified, by Chad Savage

Published by Three Moons Media
2300 Bill Owens Parkway #928
Longview, Texas 75604-3059

http://www.threemoonsmedia.com

Printed in the United States of America

ISBN 0-9725164-4-1

Dedicated to my love, Wendy,
and our children.

With a special thank-you to Llana and Burr
for the green quiet of their home,
and to my friend James for the comic relief.

I wish to also thank Three Moons Media
for making this book a reality.

To touch the dragon you must reach past your fear of failure!

See in yourself the perfect you.

It is always there...but sometimes, we forget.

Like a diamond of light...

See it reflected in the eyes of your dragon...

Know that you are a perfect star!

To touch the dragon you must surrender to your greatness!

Note to self, 6/16/94

Contents

Foreword	xiii

Part I :: Here There Be Dragons — 1

Prologue and Caution	3
Chapter One :: *Dragons of Sacred Space*	5
Enter the Dragons ::	6
In the Heart of Sacred Space Dwells the Altar ::	7
Calling the Dragons ::	9
Chakras from the Occidental Perspective ::	10
Magick ::	13
Dragon Magick ::	13
Chapter Two :: *The Dragon of the Sea*	15
Those That Came Before ::	16
Shrine of Things Gone By ::	17
Selected Celtic Deities ::	17
Magick of the Dragon of Sea ::	18

Chapter Three :: *The Dragon of Land*   21
   Touching the Earth ::   21
   What are these Watchtowers? ::   22
   Dragons of the Quarters ::   23
   Selected Celtic Deities ::   23
   Magick of the Dragon of Land ::   23

Chapter Four :: *The Dragon of Sky*   25
   Things to Come ::   25
   Selected Celtic Deities ::   27
   Shining Ones of Night and Day ::   27
   Magick of the Dragon of Sky ::   28

Chapter Five :: *Sacred Flame*   33
   Let there be Darkness ::   34
   Let there be Light ::   35
   Selected Celtic Deities ::   36

Part II :: The Book of Dragon Shadows   39

Draconic Charge of the Goddess ::   43
Draconic Charge of the God ::   45
Draconic Code ::   47
Alternate Wiccan Rede ::   47
Chant of the Alchemist's Dragon ::   49
The Altar ::   51
Circle of Dragons ::   53
Invoking the Lord and Lady ::   57
Enochian Keys 1 and 2 ::   59
Enter the Dragon Realm ::   65
Draconic Cone of Power ::   67
Esbat : Drawing Down the Moon ::   71

Sabbats ::	75
The Great Rite ::	77
To Touch a Dragon ::	79
The Dragon Staff ::	83
Dragon Magick Consecration ::	85
Dragon Staff Attunement ::	87
The Path to the Sea ::	91
The Lords of Land and Nature ::	95
To Touch the Clouds ::	99
Dancing in the Flames ::	105
Fire, Oil and Smoke ::	109
Magickal Spells ::	123

Afterword — 145

Appendices — 147
- A :: Tarot (Major Arcana) Impressions :: — 149
- B :: Ogham :: — 150
- C :: Phases of the Moon :: — 151
  - Three Faces, Four Quarters and the Moon :: — 152
- D :: Banishing and Invoking Pentagrams :: — 155
- E :: English of the Enochian Keys :: — 156
- F :: Dragons, Selected Celtic Deities and other Notes :: — 157

Bibliography — 161

Foreword

Sea, Land, Sky: A Dragon Magick Grimoire is about Dragon Magick, but even more, it is about the realms where magick can, and should take place. In **Part I,** *Here There Be Dragons,* you are introduced to the world of Dragon Magick, and the Realms of Sea, Land, and Sky. Here there be dragons, and here you will learn the mystical art of meeting them, and how to incorporate them into your magickal rituals. In **Part II,** *The Book of Dragon Shadows,* you will discover a miscellany of rituals, spells, and formulas. Everything needed to practice the art of Dragon Magick.

It should be noted, this book is not for the novice. You need to already have a basic understanding of your path. A firm grasp on how to create Sacred Space (cast a circle), and your own connection with Deity. If you are seeking a primary book, I would recommend *The Craft: Grimoire of Eclectic Magick,* which can be downloaded as a free e-book from my website (http://www.eclecticmagick.com/thecraft). Some may notice minor differences in information between the two books. This is in a large part due to a greater understanding of the subject matter by this writer at this time.

This book has been designed to be used by the solitary witch, or by a group.

Visit http://www.eclecticmagick.com/sealandsky for updates and additions to this book.

Sea, Land, Sky :: Part I

Here There Be Dragons

Prologue and Caution

Dragons: you find them everywhere. From Tiamat of Assyro-Babylonian mythology to the Leviathan of the Hebrews (Book of Isaiah chapter 27). There are the dragons of Chinese culture, and myth. The Vikings had their dragons, the Aztecs also had a dragon. Dragons are found almost every place that man is found. We seem to have some primal archetypal link with these giant creatures.

Could dragons just be an afterimage trapped in our cultural memory from some distant pre-man that glimpsed the last of the race of some long-dead creature? Or are dragons something more than memory? Could it be that they co-exist with us in a dimension that dreams, and magick give us access to?

Whatever the case, whatever your belief, I submit that with knowledge, and practice, you can employ dragons in your magick. Yes, this is a book about Dragon Magick.

This book is not designed for the beginner!

For this book to be of value to you, it is presupposed that you have a working knowledge of the four-element system common to most Western Magickal systems. That you have mastered the basics of creating Sacred Space, or casting a circle. You have your own Deities, tools, and are following some form of Wicca, Neo-Wicca, or Wiccan-derived Neo-Pagan path.

A firm foundation on your chosen path is needed to use this book.

Any similarly between this system of magick, and any Tradition, real, or fictional, outside of that taught by the author, is strictly coincidental. Some elements that are considered as standard magickal practices, have been freely employed by the author to place the information presented in a familiar and usable format.

Chapter One

Dragons of Sacred Space

With the proliferation of books on the subjects of magick, witchcraft and Wicca in the last twenty years, almost everyone with a passing interest in the subject has in one way or another been exposed to some form of the concept of casting a circle for creating Sacred Space. To the printed information available, we can add the musical contribution of Kate Bush's song "Lily" (Red Shoes, Columbia Records 1993), and movies like "The Craft" (Columbia Pictures 1996). Anyone reading this work should already know that you call the four quarters, and that each quarter is associated with one of the four traditional (western) elements of earth, air, fire and water. Some may even be familiar with the addition of Active Spirit above and Passive Spirit below (in Wiccan concepts this would be the Sun/Sky God above and the Earth Goddess below). For most workings this creates a nice mono-dimensional bubble of Sacred Space. But what if your working requires more? How can you create Sacred Space in realms other than the one you have inherent access to?

Enter the Dragons ::

A short study of almost any philosophy will at some point present the concepts of Past, Present, and Future. To expand upon this, I put forth the following:

• Events that took place in the Past affected the shape of the Present.

•• Actions that take place in the Present affect the shape of the Future.

••• The Future is fluid and changeable.

Prior to St. George, dragons were acknowledged by many human tribes as beneficial creatures. Due to this view, the early Christian church associated the symbol of the dragon with that of the Pagan belief systems. So the act of St. George slaying the dragon was a public relations metaphor for the Christian church defeating the gods of the Old Religions. The metaphor was good, and the art created to celebrate the metaphor is beautiful. What of the reality of the church's crusade to annihilate the Old Pagan Religions? Dragons, like snakes and other reptiles, just shed their skins and return in new forms. So it is with the Old Religions: new skin, yet the same Pagan heart still beats within.

As for what the Dragon truly is, I have always felt that Merlin in the movie "Excalibur" (Warner Brothers 1981) said it best: "There coiled in the unfathomed depths, it emerges. It unfolds itself in the storm clouds, it washes its mane sparkling white in the blackness of seething whirlpools, its claws are the forks of lightning, its scales glisten in the bark of trees, its voice is heard in the hurricane, it is so much more than a scaly monster. It is Everything!"

It is a very human trait to imbue abstract concepts with personalities. This gives our minds something to grasp onto in order to better understand the concepts. To this end I introduce the Dragon of Sea (Realm of the Past), Dragon of Land (Realm of the Present), and Dragon of Sky (Realm of the Future). Each of these will be revisited in their own chapters.

With the addition of invoking the Dragons of Sea, Land, and Sky in the creation of your Sacred Space, not only will your magickal workings take place in the normal reality you have worked in before, you will also find it easier to draw from the wisdom of the past and to influence the gathering of forces for workings that affect the future. Your Sacred Space will go from the mono-dimensional sphere you are accustom to, to being a multi-dimensional junction of time and space.

In the Heart of Sacred Space Dwells the Altar ::

My friends and family have accused me of having a very minimalist approach with the layout of my altar. This could be the result of early exposure to Oriental philosophy as a teen, and twenty years in the Navy where space and privacy were a luxury. Or it could just be that I have a very minimalist approach to my altar.

So what does my altar look like?

It is composed of three ceramic bowls, an oil lamp, and my wand. The normal layout places the oil lamp in the center, and the three bowls in a triangle formation around it, with the apex pointing away from me (or North if placed in a circle). The wand is placed at the base of the triangle. As I am right-handed, the wand is pointed to the left.

The first bowl is placed in the bottom left corner of the triangle; within it is placed water. The second bowl is placed in the bottom right corner of the triangle; it holds a portion of salt. The third bowl is placed at the apex of the triangle; here is placed burning incense. The oil lamp at the center is sometimes known as a Spirit Lamp. In this system it also represents the Sacred Flame (covered in Chapter Five). The bowl of water is symbolic of the realm of Sea. The bowl of salt is for the realm of Land, and the bowl of incense is for the realm of Sky. Within this minimalist approach, all four traditional elements are present; water, earth (as salt), air (as incense), and fire (the oil lamp).

The arrangement emphases the three realms of Sea, Land, and Sky. It also projects an illustration of the relationship between the God and Goddess. The bowls of water and salt (earth), form a horizontal line across the Altar, indicative of the receptive/foundation nature of the Goddess. While the oil lamp (fire), and bowl of incense (air) form a vertical line, for the active/projectile aspect of the God

The God and Goddess are again reflected in the Spirit Lamp, where the oil (Goddess) joins with/feeds the wick (God), to produce the Sacred Flame. The two joining and becoming one, bring about Light from Darkness.

The Wand lying horizontal below the triangle of bowls, expresses the witch's (my) relationship with deity. Wands by tradition are associated with the element of Air or Fire (both of which are masculine in nature), but the Wand itself is composed of material like wood, copper, and stones that are for the most part feminine in nature. This gives the Wand a greater degree of balance then can be found in most of the other magickal weapons. This can be even more true of the Dragon Staff, when it is constructed with this balance in mind.

Please note, I am not advocating that anyone should adapt my Altar layout. It is provided only to illustrate how the Three Realm system can be integrated into a traditional (western) four-element Altar.

Calling the Dragons ::

Many systems of casting a Circle for the creation of Sacred Space require that the caster circumnavigate the outer edge of the circle a number of times to establish the boundary and begin the harmonization of the energy within the circle. The number of times that you circumnavigate the circle, can range from three up to ten depending the Tradition that it is drawn from. Some Traditions even allow that when casting very large circles, you only need to circumnavigate it once.

By utilizing this point in the ritual, you can easily integrate your personal Circle Casting with Calling the Dragons of Sea, Land, and Sky.

Adding the Three Realm system to your Circle casting

Transition...move to the North point of the Circle.

With Staff (or Wand) from the North, walk the Circle deosil chanting:

"Dragon of Sea...Guardian of the Summerland...Keeper of Forgotten Knowledge...Awake from your slumber, and join with us who remember you!" (Repeat as needed.)

Once back at the North...

With Staff (or Wand) from the North, walk the Circle deosil chanting:

"Dragon of Land...Guardian of the Earth...Keeper of Wisdom...Awake from your slumber, and join with us who remember you!" (Repeat as needed.)

Once back at the North...

With Staff (or Wand) from the North, walk the Circle deosil chanting:

"Dragon of Sky...Guardian of the Ayres...Keeper of the Wyrd...Awake from your slumber, and join with us who remember you!" (Repeat as needed.)

Once back at the North, pause for three beats of your heart, then return to the Altar...

From this point, you would proceed with the Circle Casting you normally use.

To dismiss the Dragons of the Sea, Land, and Sky, you would circumnavigate the Circle widdershins, addressing first Sky, then Land and lastly Sea. The modification you would make to the chant would be where it reads: "Awake from your slumber and join with us who remember you!" Change this to "Return to your slumber and remember us!"

Chakras from the Occidental Perspective ::

One notable element often missing in Pagan and Wiccan systems is the Chakras. What follows is my perspective of integration of common traditional western symbols, and the Chakras.

Crown chakra—Violet, Saturn, Superconsciousness
Third-Eye chakra—Indigo, Moon, Intuition
Throat chakra—Blue, Mercury, Communication
Heart chakra—Green, Venus, Love/Healing
Solar Plexus chakra—Yellow, Sun, Personal Power
Abdominal chakra—Orange, Jupiter, Leadership/Creativity
Root chakra—Red, Mars, Fight-Flight/Procreation

To Open Your Chakras

Sit in a comfortable chair, lie on the floor, or stand, then slow your breathing. Visualize each of the chakras as an egg of the appropriate color.

Take a deep breath, visualize it as red, see it flow down your body until it reaches the red egg. As you exhale, see the red egg hatching, and a small red dragon fly out with your exhaled breath.

Take a deep breath, visualize it as orange, see it flow down your body until it reaches the orange egg. As you exhale, see the orange egg hatching, and a small orange dragon fly out with your exhaled breath.

Take a deep breath, visualize it as yellow, see it flow down your body until it reaches the yellow egg. As you exhale, see the yellow egg hatching, and a small yellow dragon fly out with your exhaled breath.

Take a deep breath, visualize it as green, see it flow down your body until it reaches the green egg. As you exhale, see the green egg hatching, and a small green dragon fly out with your exhaled breath.

Take a deep breath, visualize it as blue, see it flow down your body until it reaches the blue egg. As you exhale, see the blue egg hatching, and a small blue dragon fly out with your exhaled breath.

Take a deep breath, visualize it as indigo, see it flow into your head until it reaches the indigo egg. As you exhale, see the indigo egg hatching, and a small indigo dragon fly out with your exhaled breath.

Take a deep breath, visualize it as violet see it flow up until it reaches the violet egg. As you exhale, see the violet egg hatching, and a small violet dragon fly out with your exhaled breath.

Take a deep breath, visualize it as white, see it flow down your body until it reaches your feet. As you exhale, see the seven colored dragons flying around your body forming an egg of white light.

To Close Your Chakras

Sit in a comfortable chair, lie on the floor, or stand, then slow your breathing. Visualize the seven colored dragons flying around your body forming an egg of white light.

Focus upon the violet dragon. Take a deep breath, visualize the violet dragon flying into your body to the place where the violet egg was. As you exhale, see the violet dragon returning to sleep and the egg reforming around it.

Focus upon the indigo dragon. Take a deep breath, visualize the indigo dragon flying into your body to the place where the indigo egg was. As you exhale, see the indigo dragon returning to sleep and the egg reforming around it.

Focus upon the blue dragon. Take a deep breath, visualize the blue dragon flying into your body to the place where the blue egg was. As you exhale, see the blue dragon returning to sleep and the egg reforming around it.

Focus upon the green dragon. Take a deep breath, visualize the green dragon flying into your body to the place where the green egg was. As you exhale, see the green dragon returning to sleep and the egg reforming around it.

Focus upon the yellow dragon. Take a deep breath, visualize the yellow dragon flying into your body to the place where the yellow egg was. As you exhale, see the yellow dragon returning to sleep and the egg reforming around it.

Focus upon the orange dragon. Take a deep breath, visualize the orange dragon flying into your body to the place where the orange egg was. As you exhale, see the orange dragon returning to sleep and the egg reforming around it.

Focus upon the red dragon. Take a deep breath, visualize the red dragon flying into your body to the place where the red egg was. As you exhale, see the red dragon returning to sleep and the egg reforming around it.

Take a final deep breath. As you exhale see the energy that you had raised returning to the earth below.

Once you have mastered this method, you can use it to add energy to your spell and ritual work by waking only the appropriate dragon within you.

Magick ::

Aleister Crowley said, "Magick is the Science and Art of causing Change to occur in conformity with Will."

The practice of magick in any form is not for the weak willed. This is not a place for parlor games, it is a discipline for those who are masters of their own realities. If you are unable, or unwilling to accept the consequences of your actions, you have no business stepping into a circle, and creating Sacred Space. Every act of magick has a price. You cannot seek to make deals with the universe.

When you choose to step into the circle, and practice magick, you are in effect saying to the universe, "I freely and willingly take on the responsibilities for my actions. I unconditionally accept the price required to have my Will made Manifest!"

Dragon Magick ::

So, what is Dragon Magick, and what makes it any different from any other form of magick?

Dragon Magick is not High Magick, nor is it Low Magick. It has been the experience of this writer that in reality there is very little difference between these two so-called forms of magick, in the same way that so called Black and White magick are just vain attempts by the employer to justify their actions without fully accepting responsibilities for those actions. All magick is grey! How you use it and what form it takes is a matter of your ethics. No one else's, just yours!

When you seek to employ dragons in your magickal workings, you are seeking to go beyond the conscious mind and tap into the primal archetypes of the subconscious and superconscious minds. Each person has the ability to suspend their belief in the physical reality and step into the vast untapped vistas of the subconscious mind. This is the space that artists and inventors dance in. The place where what is, what was, and what could be merge into a plateau of possibilities. The superconscious mind is that which is also known as God-consciousness. It is where all things are connected. In Star Wars (Lucas Film Ltd., 1977) they call it the Force.

For the purposes of this work, think of these three forms of consciousness in this manner:

Dragon of Sea—subconscious mind

Dragon of Land—conscious mind

Dragon of Sky—superconscious mind

With the act of summoning the Dragons of Sea, Land, and Sky you are reaching back into the primal abyss and forward into the unfathomable future.

Chapter Two

The Dragon of Sea

The Dragon of the Sea (Realm of Past) represents archetype primal forces, like chaos and order. From this space are also manifest our ancestral spirits and tribal devic energy patterns.

If the Dragon of the Sea dwells in the past, how then can we connect with it?

Lucky for us, the subconscious part of our brain has no concept of the meaning of time. In the broader aspects of this concept it means simply that time is a man-made creation, in his attempt to control his environment. In the finer aspects, it means by suspending our belief that time is an absolute barrier, we can access information from days gone by. In many ways, each time we create Sacred Space we are doing this very thing.

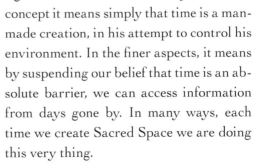

I am not implying that we have the ability to go back in time and change events that have already taken place. What I am saying is that with practice, we can learn details of those events that we had no conscious knowledge of before.

Those That Came Before ::

Each of us is the sum-total of our ancestors. We know that our DNA is a composite of our father's DNA and our mother's DNA. Unless we have an identical twin, our DNA is unique to us. In the same way, our personality is a composite of our parents, our environment, and our culture.

There is also the belief that we retain the memories of our ancestors encoded in our DNA, as well as our Tribal/Clan memories. Add to this mix the belief that we have access to the memories of our past lives. With each past life comes the collection of their ancestral and Tribal/Clan memories. The net becomes larger, and larger, and the possible information accessible quickly moves towards the range of the infinite.

To help you visualize this collection of memories, use the now-familiar metaphor of the Internet. The interface between your conscious mind and your subconscious mind is like that of a web browser. Finding what you seek is a simple matter of inputting the correct search parameters into your psychic search engine. With time and practice you will soon be capable of accessing information from the collective subconscious of your DNA.

Many old-world and oriental cultures place a great deal of emphasis upon honoring their ancestors. In the instant gratification mentality of the modern world, we often forget to stop and remember all those who came before us. It was their work, dreams, and blood that created the world we now live in. The best that our society has to offer them are monuments that after a generation or two have little or no meaning for those who take the time to stop and view them.

Shrine of Things Gone By ::

Our ancestors are always with us; we carry them in our very DNA. With the act of creating a shrine to honor our ancestors, we are honoring ourselves. Some families already have a shrine, though they might not think of it in those terms. It could be a collection of old photos on a piano, a wall covered with mementos and photos, or it could be just a single item placed on a shelf by itself. Whatever form it takes, it is in my opinion an important aspect of every magickal path.

If you don't already have a Shrine of Things Gone By, you should make one. The shrine need not be complex, simply a place for a candle and perhaps a photo or memento of someone who has passed over. When you find the stress of the modern world getting the better of you, sit before your shrine. Light a candle and allow your ancestors to take you back to a time when life was less complex. Draw strength from them; find peace with them, and within you.

Selected Celtic Deities ::

MANANNAN: (Irish, Manx, Welsh) Alternate spelling Manann. Sea God with chameleon-like nature. Call upon him when you have need of the power of release. Meditate upon him when you seek to sail upon the stream of your own consciousness.

FAND: (Irish, Manx) Sea Goddess and faery queen. Call upon her when you seek responsible pleasure without guilt. Meditate upon her when seeking to gain control over emotional responses.

Magick of the Dragon of Sea ::

The magick of this realm falls into two basic categories: divination or communication with the dead, and the more prohibited arts of necromancy and necrophilia. For anyone seeking a greater understanding of magickal necrophilia, the writings of Leilah Wendell are highly recommended. (http://www.westgatenecromantic.com/)

Television shows like "Crossing Over with John Edward" have helped in bring about a greater acceptance of those gifted in the art of channeling the communications of the dead. The rash of psychic hot-lines exhibit the public's willingness to ac-

cept the possible reality of the arts of divination. Now if we could just get all of the quacks and con-artists off the phones!

Every user of the magickal arts, should be a master of one form of divination or another. Be it the Tarot, Runes, or just reading tea leaves, we all need a system to aid us in the interpretation of events around us. A way, if you will, to step back and look at the subject from a different viewpoint.

One tool often overlooked in today's world is the magickal black mirror. A short list of books on the subject:

Clough, Nigel R., *How to make and use Magic Mirrors*, Samuel Weiser Inc., 1977

Jade, *The Magic Mirror Book*, Eye of the Cat (Long Beach, CA), 1990

Katlyn, *The Art of Scrying and the Magick Mirror*, Mermade Magickal Arts, 1989

Tyson, Donald, *How To Make and Use a Magic Mirror—Psychic Windows into New Worlds*, Llewellyn Publications, 1990

If you do not wish to go through the work of creating your own magickal black mirror, you might check with your local occult shop, or contact The Eye of the Cat (http://eyeofthecat.com) in Long Beach, CA. At one time magickal mirrors could be found for sale there.

Chapter Three

The Dragon of Land

The Dragon of the Land (Realm of Present) represents the Life Force of the earth and infuses every aspect of the physical and non-physical world. From this space are also manifest the dryads and genus locurum of our world.

Touching the Earth ::

In many ways cities have disconnected us from the flow of natural energies. The layers of concrete, steel, pipes, and wires have generated an artificial reality where more and more people dwell. For followers of many of the Pagan paths, this can lead to a feeling of being disconnected. The possible remedy to this problem is very simple. Get back in touch with the soil. Visit a park, take a trip to the country, or just plant a window box and grow some plants in your home.

The act of working with the soil places you back in contact with the natural energies of the earth. Dig your fingers into the cool dampness, close your eyes, and see the soil with the tips of your fingers. Pick plants that fit into your lifestyle—a window herb box for a homebody, or if you always seem to be on the go, grow a cactus.

Take the time to learn about the plants that are native to where you live. Find and explore the parks in your city. How many of those native plants still survive there?

Many cities even have botanical gardens, where you can see and experience exotic plants from all over the world. Take the time to reconnect with nature. After all, you are a follower of a nature religion; you should be in touch with the body of your Goddess.

The Dragon of Land is every aspect of the world we live in daily. From the soil, stones, plants, and trees, to the very fabric of the buildings that make up our cities. The Dragon of Land is also the eternal "now!" To advance one's abilities in magick, you must be the master of the moment. The ability to be here now, slowing the mind to focus upon the moment. Not having part of your brain worrying about what needs to be done tomorrow, or dwelling on the mistakes of yesterday. For in reality, this moment is all that there really is. It would be a real shame if you missed it.

What are these Watchtowers? ::

Ever ask yourself where the Watchtowers found in so many Wiccan and Pagan rituals come from? We modern Pagans got them courtesy of the rituals of the Golden Dawn. They in turn took them from medieval grimoires. It seems that back in the days when the world was still flat, it was an accepted belief that at the four corners of the world stood great watchtowers where the winds lived and where Archangels stood and watched over mankind.

The world is now round, and most of us know that the winds are generated by the relationship between high and low pressure systems in the atmosphere. So why invoke watchtowers and Archangels in your rituals?

Dragons of the Quarters ::

Well, this is dragon magick, so it only makes sense to have dragons at the four quarters. Please note that the following associations are based upon the most common system in use. If you subscribe to another arrangement, feel free to make the changes necessary to work with your system.

In the East say, "Dragon of the East, Guardian of Air, Keeper of Knowledge, Be Here Now!"

In the South say, "Dragon of the South, Guardian of Fire, Keeper of Boldness, Be Here Now!"

In the West say, "Dragon of the West, Guardian of Water, Keeper of Valor, Be Here Now!"

In the North, "Dragon of the North, Guardian of Earth, Keeper of Silence, Be Here Now!"

To dismiss, change "Be Here Now!" to "Depart In Peace!"

Selected Celtic Deities ::

DAGDA: (Irish) Alternate spelling Daghdha. Principal deity of the Tuatha De Danann. Father Nature.

DANU: (Irish) Alternate spelling Dana, also Don (Welsh). First great mother Goddess of Ireland. Mother Nature.

Magick of the Dragon of Land ::

Here we have curses, cures, potions, hexes, spells, brews, and what Scott Cunningham called "natural magic." This is the realm that most, if not all of us, think of when we talk about Witchcraft and magick. This is the realm where we practice the art of Thaumaturgy. Thaumaturgy is any attempt to influence events in your environment.

The rules that govern this realm are known by many names. They are composed of concepts like "what goes around, comes around," and ""like attracts like."

When practicing the arts of Thaumaturgy a balance must be kept in all things. Moderation is the key to success in your magickal workings. Never seek more then you need. Never acquire more power then you have a use for. Always remember that you can only go as fast as your slowest horse. A wise witch always knows how fast their slowest horse can travel.

It is often the case with thaumaturgy that intent and desire are as much a factor in the success of a spell as any other element used in the working. After all, magick takes place first in the mind, then in the physical world. This is how the witches influence events and have their will prevail over the physical world. Anyone who thinks that magickal spells are anything but inflicting their pleasure over the environment, and that of the will of others, should not be practicing magick in the first place.

Chapter Four

The Dragon of Sky

The Dragon of the Sky (Realm of Future) is symbolic of the refined archetype patterns of the Gods, and Goddesses. From this space also manifest the Sidhe, and demigods of legend

Things to Come ::

Ever want to know what is waiting for you after your alarm wakes you up in the morning? Wouldn't it be nice if you could get a feel for the events of the day, before your morning coffee? Well, you are a witch, what is stopping you from doing just that?

Many systems of magickal training require you to do some form of forecasting each day. This is often performed by the use of the I Ching (or Yi King), Runes, or the Tarot. I myself have even employed Goddess Stones and various motivational card decks.

The I Ching is a system where you toss three coins six times to create a hexagram. This hexagram will be one of sixty-four, each of which has a unique cryptic meaning. Back in 1979, I noticed that the I Ching is binary in nature, much like our modern computers. The whole pattern can be laid out on a chess board, and the hexagrams have names and relationships like a family.

The downside (for me) was that the I Ching meanings are so cryptic that the relationships between the hexagrams and my day were never apparent until after the day was done. For this reason and others, I chose to learn and use the Tarot for forecasting daily events.

How to use the Tarot to do a forecasting (outline)
   1—Clear your mind
   2—Draw a card
   3—Derive a meaning from the card.
   4—Write down your impression

Okay, that sounds too simple. First off, how do you clear your mind?

I have found by trial and error that the best method for me is to take a deep breath, and as I exhale I use my hands to push down into the earth all of the background noise in my mind. Then I think about a blank piece of paper. This works for me, as I always go blank when I sit down to write a letter to my mother.

Next you draw a card. If you are not a Tarot wizard, I would recommend using only the major arcana to start with. Shuffle the deck before you start and lay the cards out face down. If you close your eyes when you clear your mind. Then when you open your eyes, you should find that you are drawn to one of the cards, more then to the others. Pick it up, and turn it over. (Personal note, I do not use reverse meanings of the cards for this method.)

All right, now you have this card; what does it mean? If you think about what you know the day ahead holds for you and then look at a list of keywords for that card, some of the words should be more applicable then others. Write down what you think these keywords mean. Then in the evening (or when your day is done), review what you wrote down before and make note of what, if any, relationship there was with your day. You might also wish to review the keywords again and a list of meanings associated with that card.

With practice, your subconscious mind can be trained to deliver the information you are seeking in a format you can recognize, and use. (For your enjoyment, in Appendix A, I have included a list of my impressions about the major arcana.)

Selected Celtic Deities ::

LUGH: (Pan-Celtic) Alternate spellings Lamhfada, also Lugus (Breton, Continental), and Llew (Welsh). Primary deity of the Druids. It is said that he had a earthly father; this aspect makes him a bridge between the mortal realm, and the realm of the divine. Within him the forces of light and the forces of darkness are in balance.

BRIDGET: (Irish, Scottish) Alternate spellings Brid, Bride, Brigit, Brighid, also Brigindo (Continental), related to Brigantia and Brittania (Anglo-Celtic). The supernal mother Goddess. The sovereign Goddess of Ireland (and Great Britain as Brittania). Bridget is the spiritual fire of creativity.

Shining Ones of Night and Day ::

Your relationship with your deities is as important as any other aspect of your magickal life. It was presupposed at the beginning of this work that you already have a relationship with the gods. They are a key to how magick works and to how you perceive the world around you. If you do not already have a strong relationship with the gods, you need to create one.

While I was in the Navy, I spent a year on Diego Garcia. It was for me a time to renew my relationship with the gods. The Goddess would wake me at 2 AM on nights of the full moon with a craving for chili fries. The Green Man would walk with me in the jungle, and the two of them would dance with me by the sea. For a time, I learned to view the world with different eyes.

I was lucky; not everyone can spend a year on a tropical island in the Indian Ocean, just to reconnect with their gods. Yet everyone can take the time to observe the interaction that takes place in nature. Even in large cities there are unique relationships between the world of man and the actions of the gods. Look up and see the birds. Many cities even have hawks floating on the wind between the skyscrapers.

Remember the gods, and they will remember you.

Magick of the Dragon of Sky ::

The magick of this realm falls into two groups. The first of these are the rituals and rites of Theurgy, that is, rituals that have a strong religious nature. The second type of magick of this realm are those spells and workings that seek to influence future events.

To Draw Down the Moon

Traditional religions imply that only a member of the clergy has a right to call upon the deity. One of the greatest appeals that Wiccan and Pagan paths offered when they first made their mass-market appearances in the 1970s was the right of every initiate to invoke the Goddess. This is often known as drawing down the moon.

As with most of the rituals in this book, the following is presented for use by the solitary witch, but can be easily adopted for group workings.

Lunar Tide: Full Moon (100 percent illumination) at the zenith
Needed
   :: basic Altar
   :: magickal black mirror (or silver bowl with clean water)
   :: incense—Vision (see Part II: Oil, Fire, and Smoke)

Having cast the circle and called your deities, stand facing the altar so that the moon is in front of you.

Give the sign of water and perform the chakra-opening exercise given in Chapter One.

Say, "Tiamat about me burning bright. (With the right hand touch to the right of the Heart chakra) Tiamat (touch to the left of the Heart chakra) within me (touch the Abdominal chakra) give me (return to the right of the Heart chakra) sight."

Raise your hands up in the sign of Greeting the Goddess and recite the Draconic Charge of the Goddess (see Book of Dragon Shadows) while looking at the moon. Then lower your arms and look into the black magick mirror. If it is the desire of the Goddess for you to receive a vision, it will be in the black mirror. If you have a request of the Goddess, now is the time to ask.

Close the ritual as you have skill and knowledge to do.

The Magick of Tarot

Not only can Tarot cards be used to read the future, in the hands of a skilled witch, they can be use to create the future. With an intuitive understanding of the cards' meanings, a pattern can be established to focus the forces of the universe towards your goal.

The system can be simple or as complex as you choose to make it. You must first have a full understanding of the issue, the obstacles, the ultimate goal, and the type of energy needed to achieve that goal.

To show how this might be done, we will use an example of an upcoming job interview. For this spell, we will use a simple three-card layout. The card on the left will represent the past, or everything that has taken place up to this time. The second card, placed in the center, will represent the present or obstacle. The final card, placed to the right, will be the future we are seeking to manifest.

Example: For the first card, use the 5 of Pentacles (Loss; unpleasant disagreements) if you lost your job, or the 7 of Pentacles (progress halted) if you are seeking a new/better job, but are still working. You could even use the 4 of Cups (dissatisfaction) if you are just unhappy at you current job.

Example: For the second card, use the 7 of Wands (competition) if there are a number of others also applying for the same job, or if you are just nervous about the interview, use the 2 of Swords (tension, or indecision). Try the 5 of Swords (slander, or failure) if you were fired under questionable circumstances.

Example: For the final card, use the 2 of Pentacles (harmony through change), 8 of Pentacles (new opportunities), King of

Pentacles (success in business), or the Ace of Pentacles (material success).

Even for a simple example, there are a lot of choices. Let us narrow this down some and say that you are still working, but are seeking a better position, and you are a little nervous about the interview. The first card would be 4 of Cups (dissatisfaction), the second card 2 of Swords (tension, or indecision), and the third card 8 of Pentacles (new opportunities). Add to this a green candle, and some calming incense, like copal, or sandalwood.

Lay out the cards, light the incense and candle, clear your mind, and state clearly your desired outcome. As this working deals with money, it should be done once each day for the four days before the interview.

To elaborate upon this system, making it more complex, you would expand upon the first and second card positions with additional cards to create an accurate picture of those placements. You should only use one card in the third position, as this is where you are focusing your energy, and with magick, the forces of the universe.

Chapter Five

Sacred Flame

Along with the Three Realms, Four Elements, and all of the various possible elementals, there is also the Sacred Flame (not to be confused with the Element of Fire). The Sacred Flame exists as an essential part of all of the Realms, Elements, and elementals. It is the spark of the divine that flows through all of nature. The Sacred Flame is that from which all

things draw spirit, and to which all things will return. The Sacred Flame is symbolized as the genus locurum of the First Dragon.

This is the glue that binds all things together: the Tao of

ancient China, the Holy Ghost of the early Christians, the Force of the Star Wars movie series. It exists in all things and makes all things one. If you did not know already, everything is connected.

Let there be Darkness ::

Samhain :: October 31

The last day of summer. The Goddess descends into the Dark Lord's realm, and the Green Man lays sleeping in the fields. This was the old Celtic New Year, when the veil was thinnest between realms.

This was the night when the Great Ride took place, and any who had passed over and were still lingering in this realm were called to dine at the Dark Lord's cauldron.

A simple Samhain ritual for the solitary Witch

Needed: Dinner table, large bowl of stew, spoons, and small bowls as needed, other items as you deem required.

Time: 11 PM on October 31

Beforehand, make some stew or soup. Set the table for yourself, the God, and Goddess, and a place for anyone you knew who has passed into the Summerland in the last twelve months. You can also set places for any one who has passed over that you might desire to have a conversation with.

The ritual: Cast your circle around the table. Invoke the God, and Goddess as you know how. Perform the chakra-opening exercise, then serve the stew in a deosil manner around the table, greeting each guest as you do. Serve yourself last. Bless the meal, then be seated, eat, drink, and visit with your guest.

At the end of the meal, thank each of your guests for coming, Thank the God and Goddess for being there. Perform the chakra-closing exercise, then close the circle. Do not forget to clear the table and do the dishes.

Let there be Light ::

Beltain :: May 1

The first day of summer. The Goddess ascends from the Dark Lord's realm, and the Green Man dances in the fields. It is a time of celebration, and joy. In the old days, it was a time when the gods would take possession of bodies, and encourage the crops to grow.

Besides dancing around the May Pole and rampant sexual license, it was a time of new light, a time when the sacred Bel fire was kindled; from which each family would take home a part to rekindle their hearth fires.

A simple Beltain ritual for the solitary Witch

Needed: Bathtub, water, floating candle(s), other items as you deem required.

Time: Sunset on May 1

Before the ritual: On the bottom of each floating candle carve a wish that you would like granted during the coming year. Fill the bathtub with warm water, add salt and herbs to your liking.

The ritual: Cast a circle around the room, light incense, put out all sources of light. Step into the bathtub and sit down. Perform the chakra-opening exercise, then in the darkness pick up your floating candle (or the first if you have more then one), and light it saying "Goddess grant my request!" (Repeat as needed.)

Sit in the water and watch the floating candle(s) burning.

When the water begins to get too cold, it is time to get out of the tub. Remember to close your chakras and the circle before leaving the room.

Selected Celtic Deities ::

TALIESIN: (Pan-Celtic) Son of the Goddess Cerridwen. Master of non-linear time, and guardian of tradition and secrecy.

CERRIDWEN: (Scottish, Welsh) A crone mother Goddess

famous for "Amen" her great cauldron of knowledge. She is the embodiment of wisdom gained through trial, transformation and the quest within.

Taliesin, Cerridwen, and the cauldron Amen form a symbiotic relationship that illustrates the concept of the Sacred Flame. Amen is the physical container that holds the oil. Cerridwen is the oil, both as the mother giving birth and as the crone transforming the oil into the flame. Taliesin is the flame, giving light, guidance, and the willingness to sacrifice all to achieve knowledge/wisdom/skill.

Sea, Land, Sky :: Part II

The Book of Dragon Shadows

Birth Name:
Birth Date:
Sun sign:
Moon sign:
Craft Name:
God:
Goddess:
Dedication:
Vision ~ To Touch a Dragon:
Dragon Staff created:
Dragon Staff consecrated:
Dragon Staff attunement:
Vision ~ Path to the Sea:
Vision ~ Lords of Land and Nature:
Vision ~ To Touch the Clouds:
Vision ~ Dancing in the Flame:
Other Special Dates:

Draconic Charge of the Goddess ::

I am the heart of darkness
I am the soul of night
I am the virgin earth
I am life, and love, and light

Know me in the wild wind
Know me in the sea
Know me in a lone bird's call
Know me and be free

I am the unformed chaos
I am the mother prime
I am the Dragon Goddess
I am all of space and time

Know me in the kiss of death
Know me in the heat of lust
Know me in the cry of birth
Know me in perfect love and trust

I ask not for your life
I ask not for your soul
I ask only you remember me
In moon tides new and full

I am the source of all light
I am the creatrix of days
I am the Mother Earth
I am with you in all ways

Draconic Charge of the God ::

In the lonely places you'll find me
Where standing stones greet the moon
In the quiet places you'll know me
At dusk, midnight, dawn, and noon

I am the rider of the storm
I am lightning, rock and tree
I am the leader of the hunt
I am the wolf, the hawk, the bee

At conception I was with you
In the darkness of the womb
And in death I will greet you
When you lie in your tomb

I am the Green Man in the Spring
I am the Horned God in the Fall
I am the Spirit of each season
I am Lord of Death for all

I walk with my wing wide open
And darkness marks my path
Yet those who see the light of truth
Can always hear my laugh

And if you still don't know me
Look deep within your soul
I am the passion of desire
I'm at the end of every goal

Draconic Code ::

>My Companions are Sea, Land, and Sky
>My Shield is Reverence for Life
>My Armor is Tranquillity and Insight
>My Weapons are Fortitude and Awareness

Alternate Wiccan Rede ::

>Bide the Wiccan Laws we must
>In Perfect Love and Perfect Trust.
>Eight words the Wiccan Rede fulfil:
>"An ye harm none, do what ye will."
>Lest in thy self-defense it be,
>Ever mind the Rule of Three.
>Follow this with mind and heart,
>And merry ye meet
>And merry ye part.
>
>*—Author unknown. Source: Amber K,* Covencraft.
>*pp. 4-5. Llewellyn Publications. 1998*

Chant of the Alchemist's Dragon ::

> I arise from extinction
> I slay extinction
> And extinction slays me
> I resuscitate the corpse
> I have spawned
> And dwelling in extinction
> I annihilate myself

The Altar ::

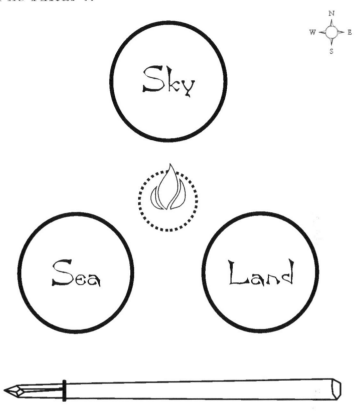

See *Part I, Chapter One:*
In the Heart of Sacred Space Dwells the Altar,
for more information.

Circle of Dragons ::

With minor changes, the following ritual presents the same steps that were given in previous sections. Before you begin, summon forth your personal dragons.

Transition...move to the North point of the Circle.

With Staff and Water circumnavigate the Circle deosil from the North, chanting:

"Dragon of Sea...Guardian of the Summerland...Keeper of Forgotten Knowledge...Awake from your slumber, and join with us who remember you!" (Repeat as needed.)

Once back at the North...

With Staff and Salt circumnavigate the Circle deosil from the North, chanting:

"Dragon of Land...Guardian of the Earth...Keeper of Wisdom...Awake from your slumber, and join with us who remember you!" (Repeat as needed.)

Once back at the North...

With Staff and Incense circumnavigate the Circle deosil from the North, chanting:

"Dragon of Sky...Guardian of the Ayres...Keeper of the Wyrd...Awake from your slumber, and join with us who remember you!" (Repeat as needed.)

Once back at the North, pause for three beats of your heart...

With Staff and Fire walk the Circle deosil from the North to the East. Once in the East make the invoking pentagram of Air:

"Dragon of the East, Guardian of Air, Keeper of Knowledge, Be Here Now!"

With the Fire, light the quarter candle.

With Staff and Fire walk the Circle deosil from the East to the South. Once in the South make the invoking pentagram of Fire:

"Dragon of the South, Guardian of Fire, Keeper of Boldness, Be Here Now!"

With the Fire, light the quarter candle.

With Staff and Fire walk the Circle deosil from the South to the West. Once in the West make the invoking pentagram of Water:

"Dragon of the West, Guardian of Water, Keeper of Valor, Be Here Now!"

With the Fire, light the quarter candle.

With Staff and Fire walk the Circle deosil from the West to the North. Once in the North make the invoking pentagram of Earth:

"Dragon of the North, Guardian of Earth, Keeper of Silence, Be Here Now!"

With the Fire, light the quarter candle.

Return to the Altar...now call down the God, and Goddess.

To dismiss the quarters, walk the Circle widdershins, use the banishing pentagram for each element, change *"Be Here Now!"* to *"Depart In Peace!"* and put out each quarter candle.

To dismiss the Dragons of the Sea, Land, and Sky, circumnavigate the Circle widdershins, addressing first Sky, then Land, and lastly Sea. Where the chant reads: *"Awake from your slumber, and join with us who remember you!"* change this to: *"Return to your slumber, and remember us!"*

Invoking the Lord, and Lady ::

It is my will, it is my right
To stand here now, within your sight
By all the power of night and day
I call the gods to come this way
Lord of Darkness, Lord of Light
Heed my call, and join this rite
Maiden, Mother, Mighty Crone
Make this space your sacred home
Now, by the names of (Goddess) and (God) I invoke thee
It is my Will, So Mote It Be!

Enochian Keys 1 and 2 ::

The Enochian Keys were received by Dr. John Dee, Royal Astrologer to Queen Elizabeth I, and Edward Kelly in 1584. On this subject, Aleister Crowley wrote, "The conjurations given by Dr. Dee are in a language called Angelic, or Enochian. Its source has hitherto baffled research, but it is a language and not a jargon, for it possesses a structure of its own, and there are traces of grammar and syntax.

"However this may be, it works. Even the beginner finds that 'things happen' when he uses it: and this is an advantage—or disadvantage!—shared by no other type of language. The rest need skill. This needs Prudence!"

The first Enochian Key should be used with workings that call upon the Dragon of Sea and the Dragon of Sky. The second Enochian Key should be used with workings that call upon the Dragon of Land. They are given below in a phonetic format for ease of use. You need only sound out the letter combinations in a chant like manner.

ENOCHIAN KEY 1

ol sonf vorsg, goho iad
balt, lonsh calz vonpho:
sobra z-ol ror i ta nazpsad
graa ta malprg: ds holq
qaa nothoa zimz, od
commah ta nobloh zien:
soba thil gnonp prge
aldi, ds urbs oboleh grsam.
casarm ohorela caba pir ds
zonrensg cab erm iadnah.
pilah farzm znurza adna
gono iadpil ds hom toh,
soba ipam lu ipamis, ds
loholo vep zomd poamal,
od bogpa aai ta piap
piamol od vooan zacare ca
od zamran: odo cicle qaa:
zorge: lap zirdo noco mad,
hoath iaida.

First Enochian Key— Phonetic Pronunciation

Oh.el Soh.neff Voh.ar.ess.geh, Goh.hoh Ee.Ah.Deh Bah.leh.teh, Loh.ness.heh Kah.el.zod Voh.neh.peh.hoh:

Soh.beh.rah Zod Oh.el Roh.ar Ee Tah Nah.zod.pess.ah.deh Gar.ah.ah Tah Mah.el.par.geh:

Dess Hoh.el.que Que.ah.ah Noh.teh.hoh.ah Zod.ee.meh.zod, Oh.deh Koh.meh.mah.heh Tah Noh.beh.loh.heh Zod.ee.el.neh: Soh.bah Teh.heh.ee.el Geh.noh.neh.peh Par.gee Ah.el.deh.ee, Dess Veh.reh.bess Oh.boh.el.eh.heh Geh.reh.sah.em. Kah.sah.reh.em Oh.oh.reh.lah Kah.bah Pee.ar Deh.ess Zod .oh.nar.eh.neh.seh.geh Kah.beh Eh.rem Ee.ah.deh.nah.heh. Pee.el.ah Eff.ar.zod.em Zod.ur.zod.ah Ah.deh.nah Goh.noh Ee.ah.deh.pee.el Deh.ess Hoh.em Teh.oh, Soh.bah Ee.pah.em, Leh.uh Ee.pah.mee.ess, Deh.ess Loh.hoh.loh Veh.peh Zod.oh.em.deh Poh.ah.mah.el, Oh.deh Boh.geh.pah Ah.ah.ee Tah Pee.ah.peh Pee.ah.moh.el Oh.deh Vah.oh.ah.neh Zod.ah.kah.reh Kah Oh.deh Zod.ah.meh.rah.neh:

Oh.doh Kee.keh.el.eh Qu.ah.ah: Zod.oh.reh.geh:

Lah.peh Zod.ee.ar.doh Noh.koh Mah.deh, Hoh.ah.teh Ee.Ah.Ee.Deh.Ah

Enochian Key 2

Second Enochian Key—
Phonetic Pronunciation

Ah.deh.geh.teh   Veh.pah.ah   Zod.oh.neh.goh.meh Eff.ah.ah.ee.peh Sah.el.deh, Veh.ee.ee.veh El, Soh.bah.meh Ee.ah.el.par.geh Ee.zod.ah.zod.ah.zod Pee.ah.deh.peh:

Kah.sah.reh.mah   Ah.bar.ah.meh.geh   Tah   Tah.el.hoh Pah.rah.keh.leh.dah, Qu.tah Loh.ar.ess.el.qu Teh.veh.ar.bess Oh.oh.geh   Bah.el.toh.   Gee.vee   Keh.hee.ess   El.vess.deh Oh.reh.reh.ee, Oh.deh Mee.kah.el.peh Keh.ee.ess Bee.ah Oh.zod.oh.neh.goh.neh,   Lah.peh   Noh.ah.neh   Tar.oh.eff Koh.reh.ess Tah.geh, Oh.qu Mah.nee.neh Ee.ah.ee.don.neh. Toh.ar.zod.veh Goh.eh.el:

Zod.ah.kah.reh Kah Keh.noh.qu.oh.deh:
Zod.ah.mar.ah.neh Mee.kah.el.zod.oh:
Oh.deh Oh.zod.ah.zod.meh Var.el.peh:
Lah.peh Zod.ee.ar Ee.Oh.Ee.Ah.Deh!

Enter the Dragon Realm ::

Prior to taking up the practice of Dragon Magick, you need to dedicate yourself to that path. (This writer does not believe in self-initiations. To be initiated, you need someone else to initiate you.)

Pre-rite notes: This should be done near or on the New Moon. On the day chosen, eat once in the morning, and fast (no solid food or sugars) for the rest of the day. *If you are on a medical diet, always follow your doctor's advice!*

Bathe and meditate before time. Take with you water to drink and a pillow if desired.

Fifteen minutes before sunset, cast the your circle. Perform your chakra-opening exorcize.

Sit facing the sunset. After darkness has fallen, you can move around within the circle, but do not leave the circle for any reason.

You will be spending the night within the circle. You should record your impressions of the night in your journal.

At sunrise, sit and watch. After the sun has cleared the horizon, perform your chakra-closing exercise, banish the dragons, and close the circle.

Draconic Cone of Power ::

Step I

In a cast circle, start by standing in the north quarter of the circle (or in the east if that is your custom) facing inward. Even if you have already done so, perform the chakra-opening exercise.

Step II

Call forth your personal dragon. (The process of awakening your personal dragon is covered in "Dragon on Your Shoulder.")

Step III

Begin repeating the Chant of the Alchemist's Dragon.
After the first time, say "I am (your magickal name)!"
After the second time, say "I am one with the Dragon of Sea!"
After the third time, say "I am one with the Dragon of Land!"
After the fourth time, say "I am one with the Dragon of Sky!"
After the fifth time, say "I am one with the Lord and Lady!"

Step IV

Go on repeating the Chant of the Alchemist's Dragon, and at the same time begin moving about the circle in a deosil direction. If you are able, also begin doing spins or whirls (also in a deosil direction). Continue moving and chanting in a lazy spiral toward the center of the circle, until you are spinning about your axis at the center of the circle. When you feel that the energy of the cone is at the level you require, repeat the Chant of the Alchemist's Dragon one more time, closing with "I am one with the Sacred Flame!" Then stop chanting, and stop spinning.

Group Notes

In a group working, the HP and HPS would be the ones in the north (or east). To bring greater harmony to the working, the HP (or HPS) would verbalize the process of opening the chakras (Step I), and summoning forth the personal dragons (Step II).

In Step III, replace your magickal name with "I am one with (name of your group)!" This step would be performed by all repeating the chant, group pause while HP and HPS state the "I am etc.," followed by the group repeating the "I am etc."

In Step IV, only the HP and HPS would spiral in towards the center of the circle. Others in the group would just move, dance, spin around the edge of the circle deosil. The HP and HPS would stop spinning, raise their arms, and then state "I am one with the Sacred Flame!" This would be the indication for the rest of the group to stop moving and chanting.

Those who might have physical problems should remain in the south and just sway or do slow deosil turns while chanting. In this way they can add their energy to the cone without risk to their health.

Esbat: Drawing Down the Moon ::

The following text is basically the same as found in Part I and is placed here for easy reference.

Lunar Tide
Full Moon (100 percent illumination) at the zenith

Needed
:: basic Altar
:: Magickal Black Mirror (or silver bowl with clean water)
:: incense—Vision (see "Book of Dragon Shadows; Oil, Fire, and Smoke")

Having cast the circle, and called your deities, stand facing the altar so that the moon is in front of you.

SIGN OF WATER DETAIL

Give the sign of water, and perform your chakra-opening exercise.

Say, "Tiamat about me burning bright. (With the right hand, touch to the right of the Heart chakra) Tiamat (touch to the left of the Heart chakra) within me (touch the Abdominal chakra) give me sight." (return to the right of the Heart chakra) sight."

Raise your hands up in the sign of Greeting the Goddess and recite the Draconic Charge of the Goddess while looking at the moon. Then lower your arms, and look into the black magick mirror. If it is the desire of the Goddess for you to receive a vi-

sion, it will be in the black mirror. If you have a request of the Goddess, now is the time to ask.

Close the ritual as you have skill and knowledge to do.

Sabbats ::

There already exists a large body of works on the Sabbats. Within the realm of Dragon Magick, Beltain and Samhain are the two key Sabbats. Both of these points in the wheel of the year are hinge days: points in time and space where the veil between this realm and the realm of dragons is thinnest.

Samhain or Beltain would be a good time to start the practice of Dragon Magick. See also Part I, Chapter Five, Samhain solitary ritual (page 34) and Beltain solitary ritual (page 35).

The Great Rite ::

It is a common modern practice to perform the Great Rite symbolically, by placing the Athame into the Chalice. The following information is provided for consenting adults.

Cast the circle and establish Sacred Space within the realms of Sea, Land, and Sky. The High Priestess and High Priest are skyclad in the sight of your God and Goddess.

The High Priest gives the High Priestess the sacred Fivefold kiss, then kneels before her with his arms upraised. The High Priestess raises her arms to the sky and recites the Draconic Charge of the Goddess, then lowers her arms and reclines before the High Priest. Arms still upraised, the High Priest recites the Draconic Charge of the God, then moves over the High Priestess. Being now the vessels of the God and Goddess, the High Priest and High Priestess join together in union and become one.

The Great Rite is not something to play with. This is one ritual that should be performed with all of the sanctity that the High Priest and High Priestess are capable of invoking.

To Touch a Dragon ::

Needed
:: candle—dark maroon (or black)
:: incense—Dragon's Blood (or something extremely "earthly")
:: music (optional)—something with rain storms or distant thunder

[Note: For best results when doing a visualization of this nature, you should record the text on tape, or have someone read it to you.]

To Begin

Light the candle and incense, start the music (optional), turn off any other sources of light. Focus on the flame and relax. When you are ready, proceed with the text.

The Text

"Take three deep slow breaths...relax, and feel yourself sinking into the earth below..."

"Sink deeper...feel the earth around you...become one with the earth around you...slow your mind...slower...deeper...drifting..."

"You see before you a wooded landscape...large old primal trees tower up to the sky...a sky filled with dark rain-heavy clouds...the wind, like a gentle hand pushes you forward, and you notice a path winding into the trees...you begin to follow the path..."

"The trees loom around you blocking out the sky...you hear the sound of rain as it falls upon the boughs above...the clean damp smell of rain fills the air...the rocks that line the path you are walking down are covered with thick soft moss..."

[short pause]

"In the distance you notice a hill...as you move closer you see a cave opening...the path you are walking passes into the cave, and you find yourself following the path into the darkness..."

"Ahead of you, inside of the cave, you can make out a glow...moving towards you...the glow takes form, and you find yourself looking deep into the large eye of a dragon..."

[long pause]

"Very softly you hear a voice rumble inside your head, 'Welcome friend'...time seems to stand still as you melt into the dragon's mind...you ask, and the dragon answers your questions..."

[longer pause]

"The dragon speaks again, 'It is time for you to go.'...turning away from the glowing eye you notice an object upon a cubed stone...moving towards it, you can see that it is a Staff...you pick up the Staff, and the dragon says, 'That is for you.'...raising the Staff above your head, you feel your body rising up through the earth..."

[short pause]

"You find yourself in the here and now...you are aware of your environment...you are again in your body, opening your eyes, you are now wide awake, and refreshed."

The Dragon Staff ::

Once you have done the visualization To Touch a Dragon, (above), you will have a pattern, or at a minimum an impression of what your Dragon Staff should look like. To this, add your knowledge, and skill to create a balanced tool.

In general, the staff should be larger then a walking stick, but not taller than the witch. (Or it could be the size of a large wand.) It should be of wood. (Or it could be of metal). It might have stones, and other objects affixed to it. (Or it could be unadorned.) The only thing that can ever be truly said about the Dragon Staff is that each one is unique. Upon it should be placed the Craft name of the witch in Ogham (see Appendix B).

Once you have constructed your Dragon Staff, it will need to be consecrated.

Dragon Magick Consecration ::

This consecration can be used for other magickal weapons as well. It should be used with caution, as it tends to create interesting energy patterns that are best suited only for the use with Dragon Magick. Preliminary instructions are omitted, as it is presupposed that you know what you are doing.

Lunar Tide
   New Moon

Needed
   :: basic Altar
   :: Black Stone (or magickal black mirror, adjust the wording below as needed)
   :: incense—Vovin Cafafam (see Oil, Fire, and Smoke)
   :: source of open flame (candle, torch, or lamp)
   :: bowl of ice (loose cubes or crushed)

Having everything ready, raise the Staff before you. Bring it down upon the Black Stone, then raise it to the sky while saying, "By the Black Stone and moonless sky I consecrate this staff and give it sight."

Move the staff over the flame, then place it into the ice while saying, "With fire, and ice I give it life, by my Will I charge it thrice."

Hold the staff before you and charge it in the names of your own deities. Now breathe upon the staff three times.

Hold the staff over your head and turn deosil saying, "In the sight of the Dragons of Sky, Land, and Sea..." bring the staff down and smite the ground saying, "This is My Will, So Mote It Be!"

Finish the ritual as you have knowledge and skill to do.

Dragon Staff Attunement ::

At the first Full Moon following the consecration, the staff needs to be attuned or harmonized with the witch.

Pre-rite notes: This should be done near or on the Full Moon. On the day chosen, eat once in the morning and fast (no solid food, or sugars) for the rest of the day. *If you are on a medical diet, always follow your doctor's advice!*

Bathe and meditate before time. Take with you water to drink and a pillow if desired.

To Start the Vigil

At moon rise, cast your circle and call the Dragons as you have skill and knowledge to do. Open your chakras, take up your Dragon Staff, and begin your vigil.

Dragon on Your Shoulder

With your Dragon Staff, and the moon low on the horizon; sit in the dark and face the moon. Slow your breathing and ground your energy.

Hold the Staff at arm's length between you and the moon. Look first at the Staff, then past it to the moon. Focus upon the moon until it seems as if you are seeing the moon through the Staff. Feel the moon's energy flowing into the Staff and into your body. Spin the moonlight around you to form an egg of black and purple.

Once you can hold this image, recite the chant of the Alchemist's Dragon: "I arise from extinction. I slay extinction, and extinction slays me. I resuscitate the corpse I have spawned, and dwelling in extinction; I annihilate myself!"

Visualize the egg around you hatching. Feel the dragon's head just above yours. Feel the dragon's legs around your body.

Feel the dragon's wings behind you. Extend the wings and feel their length. Move the dragon's wings and feel the air stir around you. Fold the dragon's wings and feel the dragon merge into your body.

You have now awakened your personal dragon.

To Finish the Vigil

The vigil will be kept all night. At moonset, close your chakras, dismiss the dragons, and close your circle.

The Dragon Staff is the primary tool for the working of Dragon Magick. If possible, it should be kept wrapped in silk when not being used.

The Path to the Sea ::

Needed
:: candle—blue-green (or white)
:: incense—myrrh (or something extremely "watery")
:: music (optional)—something with ocean waves

[Note: For best results when doing a visualization of this nature, you should record the text on tape, or have someone read it to you.]

To Begin
Light the candle and incense, start the music (optional), turn off any other sources of light. Focus on the flame and relax. When you are ready proceed with the text.

The Text
"Take three deep slow breaths...relax and feel yourself sinking into the earth below..."

"Sink deeper...feel the earth around you...become one with the earth around you...slow your mind...slower...deeper...drifting..."

"You find yourself on a beach watching the tide wash upon the shoreline...slowly you walk down to the waterline...the water is warm as it flows over your feet..."

"As you enter the water, a fog rises to cover the surface...soon you are enveloped in a gentle warm blanket of mist...you drift, all of your worries and cares slowly slipping away...and you drift..."

"You hear a sound, softy at first, and then louder...looking around you see two large pearls floating in the water..."

"The fog parts, and the pearls reveal themselves to be the eyes of a dragon..."

"As you stare into the eyes you see yourself reflected...the

dragon blinks and your reflection becomes a kaleidoscope of images...you see your mother and father, and your grandparents, and a multitude of others...many are unknown, but all are familiar..."

[short pause]

"The dragon blinks again, the images vanish...You find yourself being drawn into the depths of the dragons eyes...an image beckons you down a long tunnel that seems to extend back to the beginning of time..."

[long pause]

"You hear a sound, softy at first, and then louder...You blink your eyes, and find yourself alone in the fog..."

"You feel the sand of the beach below your feet..."

[short pause]

"The fog begins to melt away, and as it does, you find yourself in the here and now...You are again in your body, opening your eyes...You are now wide awake and refreshed."

The Lords of Land and Nature ::

Needed

:: candle—dark green (or brown)
:: incense—patchouli (or something extremely "earthy")
:: music (optional)—something with Forest sounds

[Note: For best results when doing a visualization of this nature, you should record the text on tape, or have someone read it to you.]

To Begin

Light the candle, incense, start the music (optional), turn off any other sources of light. Focus on the flame and relax. When you are ready proceed with the text.

The Text

"Take three deep slow breaths...Relax and feel yourself sinking into the earth below..."

"Sink deeper...Feel the earth around you...Become one with the earth around you...Slow your mind..."

Slower...deeper...drifting..."

"You find yourself standing in the center of your Sacred Space...Around you there is a deeper vibration...Looking around you can see four large shapes standing at the four cardinal points..."

"To the East you see a dragon of Swirling Air...to the South a dragon of Blazing Fire...in the West a dragon of Rushing Water...and in the North a dragon Motionless Earth..."

[short pause]

"Voices echo and reverberate in your head...We are the Lords of Nature...We are the Dragons of Land...Know us for what we are...The four dragons flow towards you, and through you..."

[long pause]

"A single dragon now faces you...I am always with you...The dragon then returns to the form of the Lords of Nature...A mist rises around the edge of your Sacred Space...When it dissipates the dragons are gone..."

"You find yourself in the here and now...you are again in your body, opening your eyes. You are now wide awake and refreshed."

To Touch the Clouds ::

Needed

    :: candle—light blue (or white)

    :: incense—copal (or something extremely "airy")

    :: music (optional)—something with Space, or sounds of open areas

[Note: For best results when doing a visualization of this nature, you should record the text on tape, or have someone read it to you.]

To Begin

Light the candle and incense, start the music (optional), turn off any other sources of light. Focus on the flame and relax. When you are ready proceed with the text.

The Text

"Take three deep slow breaths...Relax and feel yourself sinking into the earth below..."

"Sink deeper...Feel the earth around you...Become one with the earth around you...Slow your mind...slower...deeper ...drifting..."

"You are standing upon a beach…The white sand beneath your feet is as fine and soft as baby powder..."

"Looking out to sea, you become aware that the waves are of prismatic light... As you watch, they change from red to orange, then to yellow, then green, on to blue, indigo, and finally violet..."

"Slowly the waves begin to flow higher up the beach. As they wash over your feet, you feel the sensation of lightness flow through your toes...The next wave covers you to your waist… Your legs seem to dissolve into the prismatic light..."

[short pause]

"Now the waves have covered you to your chin, your arms and chest feel as light as air...You watch as the waves flow in and cover your head...Slowly you feel yourself begin to float. After a moment you become aware that you are one with the sea of prismatic light..."

"You float weightless...All your concerns, fears, and worries just drift away...You are one with the universe..."

"Under you, you sense a movement...A stirring...Something bumps you from below..."

"Then like a ball on the nose of a seal, you are tossed into the air...As you float there, you can see a dragon rise from the prismatic sea below...You find yourself seated upon the neck of the dragon..."

"The dragon's giant wings flap three times, and you find yourself being carried upward...You watch as the beach and sea become a dot on a world slowly receding below...The moon grows larger and larger, and then you find yourself looking upon the backside of the moon with the earth sinking below the horizon..."

"The stars grow brighter, and brighter as you fly on the dragon farther into space..."

[long pause]

"After a time, you notice that one of the stars seems to be growing larger...and you hear for the first time the voice of the dragon, "We are each a star; that one is you!'..."

"The star grows larger and larger...You fly closer and closer until you find you are flying into the star itself..."

"At the heart of the star, a small island of land floats...Upon it are trees and a stream flowing gently past a lone tower...Slowly you begin to fly towards a clearing in the trees, not far from the tower..."

"The dragon lands, and you dismount and begin following a path through the trees to the tower..."

[short pause]

"At the tower, you enter and begin walking up a flight of twenty-two steps...Once at the top of the tower you find  an altar with a silver bowl of water..Looking into the bowl, you begin to see images forming like pictures on a television..."

[long pause]

"A single design forms on the surface of the bowl, you trace the design in the air over the bowl, and you hear the dragon say, 'Remember this sigil, for it holds great power for you...Looking up you see the dragon sitting on the tower wall near you...'Come, it is time to return...'"

"You find yourself again upon the dragon flying through space...After a time, a single speck of light grows brighter, and larger...Then slowly you see the world below you...The dragon flies through a cloud, and you are surrounded in a mist..."

[short pause]

"As the mist clears, you find yourself once again floating in the prismatic sea...Then the colors begin to fade, the feel of the sand is under your feet..."

"You find yourself in the here and now...You are again in your body, opening your eyes. You are now wide awake and refreshed."

[Before you forget, write down the design you saw in the silver bowl.]

Dancing in the Flame ::

Needed

:: candle—indigo (or silver, or gold)
:: incense—temple (or something extremely "sacred")
:: music (optional)—something mellow

[Note: For best results when doing a visualization of this nature, you should record the text on tape, or have someone read it to you.]

To Begin

Light the candle and incense, start the music (optional), turn off any other sources of light. Focus on the flame and relax. When you are ready proceed with the text.

The Text

"Take three deep slow breaths...Relax, and feel yourself sinking into the earth below..."

"Sink deeper...Feel the earth around you...Become one with the earth around you...Slow your mind...Slower...Deeper...Drifting..."

"You are drifting in the dark of space...Alone, and far away from anyone and anything else..."

"Time has no meaning..."

[short pause]

"After a time, you notice a silver thread flowing out of the center of your body...As your eyesight follows the thread, you begin to notice what looks like other threads...It is as if you are at the center of giant web of silver light..."

"For some unknown reason, you are stirred to reach out and grasp one of the threads...You can hear your mother's voice...You grasp another thread, and you hear the sound of your father's voice..."

"Grasping another thread, and you hear the voice of your first love speaking to you...Brushing your fingers over the threads, you hear the voices of friends and family you have known throughout life..."

[short pause]

"You notice one thread that is golden in color connected to the crown of your head...You reach up and touch it...At first there is a low hum...Slowly you discern that it is millions of voices all speaking at once, the sounds of waves breaking on a hundred reefs, rain falling in the mountains..."

"Within the hum of voices and sounds you slowly hear another voice...'I am the Divine Spark, I am the web of life, I am that which holds the universe together'..."

"Suddenly you are overwhelmed with colors, and sounds, and the feeling of being in a million places at one time..."

[short pause]

"Looking at yourself, you can see that your body is a living flame, and within that flame is a web of light connecting everything in the universe together...'I am you, and you are me, and we are everything that is'..."

[long pause]

"...'Always remember, that when you act, it is You that you are affecting'..Then there is silence, and darkness...Once again you find yourself drifting alone in the heart of space..."

[short pause]

"...Drifting...You notice that you can still faintly see the golden thread connected to the crown of your head...You reach up to touch it..."

"You find yourself back once again in the here and now...You are in your body, opening your eyes. You are now wide awake and refreshed."

Fire, Oil and Smoke ::

Candle Colors

Black: Absorbing negative energy; banishing; clearing, and cleaning; to control a bad habit; finding, or keeping a secret; New Moon, or Crone work.

Blue: Communication; throat chakra.

Blue, light: Calmness; health; patience; understanding.

Blue, dark: Change; structure.

Brown: Centering; grounding; home blessing.

Gold: God force; prosperity.

Grey: Neutrality; wisdom.

Green: Fertility; growth; healing (use with pink); prosperity; heart chakra.

Greenish-yellow: Discord; jealousy.

Indigo: Intuition; Psychic power; third-eye chakra.

Lavender: Energy control; invoking inner beauty; stress alleviation.

Mauve: Evokes cooperation; self-confidence.

Orange: Adaptability; authority; creativity; encouragement; magickal power; abdominal chakra.

Peach: Empathy; nurturing.

Pink: Friendship; harmony; healing (use with green); self-love.

Purple: Ambition; power.

Red: Anger control; passion; sexual energy; vitality/vigor; root chakra.

Silver: Emotional clarity; Goddess force; psychic clarity.

Teal: Balance; decision-making; gaining trust.

Turquoise: Learning retention; new perspective; stress alleviation.

Violet: Spirituality; The Wyrd; crown chakra.

White: Spiritual guidance; can be used as a replacement for any color.
Yellow: Confidence; intellectual control; success; solar plexus chakra.

Candle Burn Times

One hour: red; peach; pink; purple; mauve; silver; gold; violet
One hour, or until out: black; grey.
Two hours: orange; indigo; dark blue; turquoise; lavender.
Three hours: yellow; blue; light blue; teal; greenish-yellow.
Four hours, or 24 hours: green; brown.
As required: white.

Dressing a Candle

Before using candles, they should be "dressed" with oil. This is done by anointing the upper half and then the lower half.

The formulas for oils and incense are given in "parts." These are a guideline only. Experiment with the mixtures, and find the blend that works best for you.

Magickal Base Oil

Orris root
Saffron

Dragon Magick Base Oil

Dragon's Blood resin
Myrrh powder

Magickal Base oils can be used as foundation oils for other mixtures. Use a minimum of a pint of olive oil, and add the ingredients of your choice. Charge/bless the oil under a New

Moon, then set someplace cool, dark, and dry for six weeks (or under the Full Moon following the next New Moon).

The following recipes need to be blinded with 1/8 to 1/4 cup of carrier oil. Sweet almond and olive oil are recommended carrier oils. When mixing very small amounts, jojoba oil is an excellent choice. Or you can use one of the magickal base oils listed above.

Solar Oil

> 3 parts lemon
> 2 parts orange
> 1 part cinnamon
> Use for solar workings, and to clear a room of negative influences.

Lunar Oil

> 20 parts sandalwood
> 1 part jasmine
> Use for lunar workings.

Eye of Newt Oil

> 5 parts lavender
> 1 part rosemary
> 1 part ylang ylang
> Excellent blend for use on scrying tools.

Red Dragon Oil

> 5 parts dragon's blood
> 1 part rose
> For works of love.

Black Dragon Oil

   6 parts dragon's blood
   2 parts black pepper
   1 part musk
   For works of lust.

Green Dragon Oil

   4 parts cedarwood
   4 parts pine
   2 parts dragon's blood
   For works of meditation and calm healing.

Money Oil

   7 parts vetivert
   6 parts patchouli
   4 parts ginger
   3 parts cinnamon
   Use to attract prosperity.

Mystic Coffeehouse Oil

   3 parts vanilla
   1 part cinnamon
   1 part nutmeg
   espresso coffee beans (as needed)
   This one is used to raise the level of energy.

Altar Incense 1

   3 parts frankincense
   3 parts cinnamon
   1 part dragon's blood
   1 part saffron
   2 pinches golden amber resin

Altar Incense 2

    3 parts white sandalwood
    3 parts red sandalwood
    3 parts cinnamon
    1 part saffron

Both Altar Incense 1 & 2 are for general altar use. Altar Incense 1 is more suited for outdoor use, while Altar Incense 2 is best used on a daily basis inside of a room.

Beltain Incense

    5 parts eye of newt (lavendula spp.)
    3 parts rose petals
    1 part saffron

This blend is designed for use on Beltain (May 1).

Neo-Abremelin Incense

    2 parts myrrh
    1 part ginger
    1 part cinnamon

Abremelin Incense can be employed for both altar and vision (scrying) workings. The traditional formula calls for the use of "galangal" (Mars/Fire/magickal energy) which is a close relative of "ginger" (Mars/Fire/magickal energy).

Sanctuary Incense

    1 part mistletoe
    1 part juniper berries
    1 part pine needles
    1 pinch golden amber resin

This incense is best used to clean/clear a space for meditation.

Samhain Incense

> 3 parts nettles
> 3 parts cinnamon
> 1 part wormwood

This blend is designed for use on Samhain (October 31).

Temple Incense

> 3 parts frankincense
> 2 parts myrrh
> 1 part sandalwood
> 1 part eye of newt (lavendula spp.)

Use this incense to clear/clean a temple space before and after magickal workings. It can also be used for magickal workings and meditation.

Three Dragons Incense

> 3 parts kashmir
> 3 parts dragon's blood
> 2 parts myrrh

This blend has some interesting effects. It is best used for workings with the three dragons of Sea, Land, and Sky. It can also be used when doing workings for those who have crossed over and for rituals of initiation.

Vision Incense

> 3 parts wormwood
> 3 parts sandalwood
> 1 part dragon's blood
> 2 pinches golden amber resin

Use for scrying and divination workings.

Vovin Cafafam (Dragon's Abode Incense)
    2 parts dragon's blood
    2 parts red sandalwood
    1 part frankincense
    1 part cinnamon
    2 pinches golden amber resin
    a few drops vetiver oil

Use for creating sacred space for consecrations and other draconic workings.

Magickal Spells ::

A Few Notes

First, all magick and spell-casting are subjective art forms.

Second, and most important, anything worth doing is worth doing well and completely the first time.

Third, and sadly very true, the choice not to act is an act and may cause more harm than if you had acted in the first place. Many an evil has grown in power and influence because a few good people did not act when the opportunity first presented itself.

Fourth, and one I believe with all of my heart: In perfect love and perfect trust does not equal perfect doormat!

A binding is only as good as the hands that tie the knot and only as strong as the cord that holds the spell. Satin cords do not a good binding make. Use raw hemp (type) rope, the type that cuts your hands when you fashion the knots. You will be slower to cast the binding, but when you do it will last much longer.

When do we act and with what degree of force? Thin ice for sure. I do not play with love spells, as these are indeed a waste of my time and energy. I do not read Tarot cards for fun. When I reach a point where I feel the need to act, I act with all the power that is at my command.

With all spells there is a price. I act only if I am truly willing to pay that price. You cannot (and should not) cure if you can't curse. White magick is a pipe dream of the New Age Neo-Wiccan Fluffy Bunnies. All magick is grey and has a price. All help hurts someone else; all hurt helps someone else. You have to trust yourself and your gods that the path you take and the choices you make are the best options you have at that time. There is not a line set in stone; it is a wave that washes along the shore, forever changing at the whim of the moon, the sand, and the gods.

Magick is about respect! If no respect is given, then in turn no respect is received!

Money Spells

Everyone wants a spell for money. Sadly most money spells won't work. The basic problem is that money is not a goal, but it is the means to a goal. To put that statement in perspective, say you want to take a trip to another city. Instead of casting a spell to place you in the other city, you cast a spell for a road. True, you need the road to get to the other city, but the road is not the other city. The road is only the way there. Far too often when a money spell is cast, it is like creating a road, when what you really want is at the other end of the road.

For a "money spell" to be successful, you first need to be extremely clear on what you truly want. Then you must be open to the possibility that money itself, may never come into play. If you are clear and focused upon your goal, your spell has a greater chance of being successful!

The gambler who says, "Baby needs a new pair of shoes," as they roll the dice is in effect casting a money spell with a stated goal.

> Visualize a dragon sitting in a cave full of gold and silver coins.
> *Money, money come to me*
> *Money, money set me free*
> *Raise me out of poverty*
> *Money, money set me free*
> *Money, money come to me*
> *It is my Will, So Mote It Be!*

The universe does not always deliver in a straight line. You

must always be open to the opportunities as they present themselves to you. The witch who tries to put restrictions upon the universe is the witch who never sees any great return from their magick. If you cast a spell to find a better job, you must be ready and willing to move to another city.

A color version of the above graphic was posted to the cover of *The Journal of Eclectic Magick* (www.eclecticmagick.com), on February 24, 2002. The text reads "By star light, and candle bright, I cast this spell into the night. Prosperity wax; Abundance flow, bring me now unto my goal. Money, money come to me. It is my Will, So Mote It Be!" Within two weeks of posting it, various checks totaling around $300 arrived in the mail. Of that money, only about $50 was unexpected. One check for $100 was thought to have been lost, as it was over a month late. It was just the synchronicity of the universe that made the experience unique.

Prosperity Spells

When you cast a prosperity spell, you are telling the universe that you wish to raise the standard of living that you are at. In short you are saying, I am willing to pay the price so that I can have more. Sometimes prosperity spells will take a while to work. You might loose your job and be forced to move. This is just the universe trying to get you to your prosperity. If you are unwilling to move, you may never see the prosperity that you cast the spell to achieve.

There is an old saying, "The universe might not give you what you want, but she will always give you what you need."

New Car Spell

So you want a new car.

Step one: find the car you want.

Step two: get a camera and a friend, and go down to the car lot. Now pose for some photos of you in the car. (One photo of you behind the wheel is a must.)

Make copies of the photos and place them all around your home. Put one (of you behind the wheel) in the bathroom, another near your computer, one by your bed, and another on the refrigerator.

Step three: each time you go sit down in the bathroom, look at the photo of you behind the wheel of the car, and say "I look good in my car!" Always think about your car in the past tense, as if you already own it. Say to yourself, I need to get my car washed today. Last time I checked the oil it was fine.

Step four: if everything is equal, your subconscious will put into motion the events that will enable you to get the car. Once your subconscious mind thinks that you already have the car, it will move the universe to make reality fit what it perceives reality to be. In this case, you already have the car.

This method will work for other things too. Magick is a mental process.

Flying Spell

It has always been the dream of man to fly. Once this was thought to be an impossible dream. Now in many places it is something that takes place every few minutes. So why put in a spell for flying?

I don't know about you, but part of my brain just won't buy into the idea that any jumbo jet can get off of the ground and stay in the air without some kind of magickal assistance.

Just to cover all of the options, and so I can get to sleep on the flight, I always call on the help of a few dragons so that I know the jet will stay in the air. Most of the time, you never even notice that the dragons are there. If your flight is a long one, say from the west coast of the U.S. to Japan, then you might notice when the dragons change crews. There always seems to be a slight drop, what the pilot calls a minor air pocket, when one dragon lets go of the jet, and the next dragon grabs the jet, and takes over control of the flight. Some of you might be thinking that this all sounds very silly. All I know is that for over twenty years I flew all over the world, and so far I have never had a problem getting to where I was going.

Fifteen minutes before the boarding time of your flight, go into the restroom and stand before a sink with a mirror. Place your hands to your eyes, look into the mirror, and say "Dragons of Air, Dragons of the Clouds, Dragon of Sky, I call upon you to aid me on my flight. Send to me a few of your kin to keep (Name the Airline, and flight number) safe, and deliver me unharmed to (state final destination). This is my Will, So Mote It Be!" Now leave the restroom, and get on your flight.

Cloak of Invisibility

A simple spell to cast upon a shirt, jacket, or cloak. I normally use a button shirt for this spell. The item should be of silk, cotton, rayon, or some other natural fiber. The color of the item, should be grey, light tan, light blue, or black, and without any major patterns.

This spell should be cast under a New Moon for best results. Use Vovin Cafafam, or Three Dragons Incense, and a black candle. Cast your circle, open the chakra for the third-eye, and the crown, and call forth your personal dragon. Use the Second Enochian Key if you wish.

The spell is in Enochian, but can be done in English.

Phonetic Pronunciation: "Eh.teh.hah.em.zod Oh.el Ah Oh.reh.ess. Eh.oh.el Oh.el Oh.boh.el.eh Zod.ah.kah.er Ah-Ah.geh Zod.nah. Kah.er.ee.es.teh.oh.ess Ah.es.peh.teh Oh.el Ah.geh Uh.rah.neh Oh.el Zod.ah.kah.er. Zod.ee.er Ah Voh.vee.neh Zod.oh.nah.keh Geh Ree.pee.reh."

Enochian: "Ethamz ol a ors. Eol ol oboleh zacar a-ag zna. Christeos aspt ol ag de uran ol zacar. Zir a vovin zonac g ripir."

English translation: "Cover me in darkness. Make my garment move without motion. Let no one in front of me see my passage. I am the dragon clothed in no place."

Close the circle as you know how. To use the cloak/shirt, put it on and summon forth your personal dragon. Ground/center your energy, and stay focused.

Other Spells

See Part I, Chapter Four, The Magick of Tarot (page 30) for an easy-to-use system of casting almost any spell you can think up.

Afterword ::

Welcome to the edge!

You are standing upon a cliff overlooking the world, and the only thing keeping you from soaring with the dragons is the simple act of surrendering to your own greatness. We are all greater then we know. Yet when you let go of your fears, regrets, and the whole host of doubts that each of us, as humans, drag around with us on a daily basis, you will discover that you can fly.

When you surrender to your greatness, that part of you that first came into this world is set free. At birth, the Goddess made each of us a master magician. It is only life that hides this fact from us. If you can believe in dragons, they can believe in you!

Look out over the cliff, summon forth your personal dragon, stretch out your wings, and fly into the realms of Sea, Land, and Sky!

Appendices

Appendix A

Tarot (Major Arcana) Impressions :

0   The Unknown, and your Wyrd
1   Focus, control, learned knowledge, and power
2   Intuition, or dream knowledge and the Dark Goddess (Samhain to Beltain)
3   Abundance, and the Light Goddess (Beltain to Samhain)
4   Earthly power, and the Green Man (Beltain to Samhain)
5   Spiritual power, and the Horned God (Samhain to Beltain)
6   Choices, fork in the path
7   Control, balance, and understanding one's limitations
8   Courage, and inner strength
9   Inner knowledge, meditation and the conscious mind
10 Web of the Wyrd, labyrinth, change, control, and correction
11 Commitment, obligation, both in this world and the Wyrd
12 Power of water, enlightenment, and the subconscious mind
13 Transformation; new growth from old
14 Web of the Wyrd (as in pattern), connection (as in the Force from Star Wars)
15 Restrictions, chains, and limitations; only you hold the key
16 Abrupt change; renewed growth
17 Realm of the future; dragon of sky
18 Realm of the past; dragon of sea
19 Realm of the present; dragon of land
20 Reflection, awakening, and the inner voice of the super-conscious
21 Success, and the conclusion of a goal

Appendix B

Ogham ::

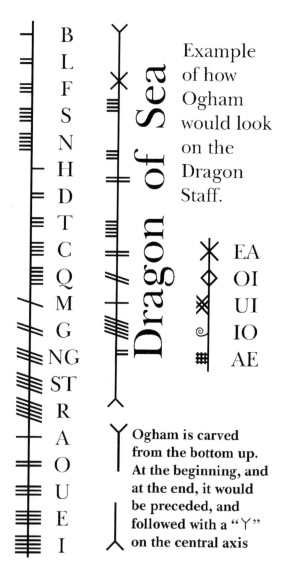

Example of how Ogham would look on the Dragon Staff.

EA
OI
UI
IO
AE

Ogham is carved from the bottom up. At the beginning, and at the end, it would be preceded, and followed with a "Y" on the central axis

Appendix C

Phases of the Moon ::

Full

2003 Jan 18, Feb 16, Mar 18, Apr 16, May 16, Jun 14, Jul 13, Aug 12, Sep 10, Oct 10, Nov 9, Dec 8.

2004 Jan 7, Feb 6, Mar 6, Apr 5, May 4, Jun 2, Jul 2, Jul 31,* Aug 30, Sep 28, Oct 28, Nov 26, Dec 26.

2005 Jan 25, Feb 24, Mar 25, Apr 24, May 23, Jun 22, Jul 21, Aug 19, Sep 18, Oct 17, Nov 16, Dec 15.

*Blue Moon

New

2003 Jan 2, Feb 1, Mar 3, Apr 1, May 1, May 31, Jun 29, Jul 29, Aug 27, Sep 26, Oct 25, Nov 23, Dec 23.

2004 Jan 21, Feb 20, Mar 20, Apr 19, May 19, Jun 17, Jul 17, Aug 16, Sep 14, Oct 14, Nov 12, Dec 12.

2005 Jan 10, Feb 8, Mar 10, Apr 8, May 8, Jun 6, Jul 6, Aug 5, Sep 3, Oct 3, Nov 2, Dec 1, Dec 31.

More detailed information can be found on the Internet from the U.S. Naval Observatory (http://aa.usno.navy.mil/data/docs/MoonPhase.html).

Three Faces, Four Quarters and the Moon :

[The following was first published on the Internet at *The Journal of Eclectic Magick* (http://www.eclecticmagick.com/moonlight.php), and is presented for reference with only minor editing.]

In 1995 while on Diego Garcia (BIOT), I was awoken a number times with the same dream/vision. I did what anyone would do, I wrote it down. Now in 2002 I have again been bothered with that same piece of information, so again I am seeking to place it into a form that can be understood by others.

If the Goddess has three faces, why do we divide her moon by quarters? This has always been one of those questions that floated someplace near the surface of my occult mind. I feel that the commonly accepted method of using the moon phases in magick leaves a lot of room for improvement. Although I cannot claim that the system I am about to put forth is the most advantageous, it does have a sound logical basis.

To understand this system, the following are deemed to be truths:

:: The Moon is a physical reflection of the Goddess and as such has certain imbued powers.

:: The Goddess has three faces, these being the Maiden, Mother and Crone.

:: A complete "lunation" (one lunar cycle) has an average duration of 29.5 days.

:: The percent of the Moon's earth-facing surface illuminated at the New Moon is 0 percent; and at the Full Moon it is 100 percent.

Before we go too far into this system you might whish to visit the U.S. Naval Observatory's website (http://aa.usno.navy.mil/data/docs/MoonPhase.html), and write down the day of the next two New Moons, and the Full Moon that falls between them. For this example I will be using the information for July of 2002. The first New Moon is on July 10, the Full Moon is on July 24, and the second New Moon is on August 8.

The first step is to take the day before, the day of, and the day after the New Moons and set them aside. In our example these would be July 9, 10 and 11 for the first New Moon, and August 7, 8 and 9 for our second New Moon. (I will come back to these).

The second step is to go to the date of the Full Moon, and count four days before, and four days after. This creates a block of nine days. In our example this would be July 20 to 23 before the Full Moon, and July 25 to 28 after the Full Moon, or July 20 to 28 for the whole block. This group of nine days is called the Mother's reign.

Now if we look above to the information we set aside before, you can see that we have two blocks of days that are so far unaccounted for. The first of these is July 12 to 19, and the other is July 29 to August 6. The days from July 12 to 19 are called the Maiden's reign, and those from July 29 to August 6 are the Crone's reign. The three days of the New Moon are called, the Dark Crone, the Dark Mother, and the Dark Maiden.

Looking at this in prospective we have in our example:

:: July 9 the Dark Crone (day before the New Moon).
:: July 10 the Dark Mother (day of the New Moon).
:: July 11 the Dark Maiden (day after the New Moon).
:: July 12 to 19 the Maiden's reign.

- :: July 20 to 28 the Mother's reign
  (four days before to four days after the Full Moon).
- :: July 29 to August 6 the Crone's reign.
- :: August 7 the Dark Crone (day before the New Moon).
- :: August 8 the Dark Mother (day of the New Moon).
- :: August 9 the Dark Maiden (day after the New Moon).

Note that the number of days in the Maiden's reign, and the Crone's reign will vary depending upon the time of year.

So what was the point of doing all of that? By better understanding the aspect of the Goddess that is being reflected by the Moon, you should be able to enhance your magick to be more in tune with the nature of the energy that is flowing through the night sky.

Appendix D

Banishing & Invoking Pentagrams ::

Banishing   **Invoking**

Appendix E

English of the Enochian Keys ::

The First Enochian Key

I reign over you, says the God of Justice, in power exalted above the firmaments of wrath: in whose hands the Sun is as a sword and the Moon is as a through-thrusting fire: which measures your garments in the midst of my vestries, and trussed you together as the palms of my hands: whose seats I garnished with the fire of gathering, and beautified your garments with admiration. To whom I made a law to govern the holy ones and delivered you a rod with the ark of knowledge. Moreover you lifted up your voices and swore [obedience and faith to him that lives and triumph] whose beginning is not, nor end can not be, which Shines as a flame in the midst of your palace, and reigns amongst you as the balance of righteousness and truth. Move, therefore, and show yourselves: open the Mysteries of your Creation: Be friendly unto me: for I am the servant of the same your God, the true worshiper of the Highest.

The Second Enochian Key

Can the wings of the winds understand your voices of wonder, O you the second of the first, whom the burning flames have framed within the depths of my Jaws; whom I have prepared as Cups for a Wedding, or as the flowers in their beauty for the Chamber of the Righteous. Stronger are your feet than barren stone, and mightier are your voices than the manifold winds. For you are become a building such as is not but in the mind of the All-Powerful. Arise, says the First: Move therefore unto his Servants: Show yourselves in power: And make me a strong Seer: for I am of him that lives forever.

Appendix F

Dragons, Selected Celtic Deities
& other Notes ::

Bibliography

Corrigan, Ian. *The Portal Book, Basic Teachings of Celtic Witchcraft*. The Association for Consciousness Exploration, 1992.

Crowley, Aleister. *Magick In Theory and Practice*. Dover Publications, Inc., New York, 1976.

Laycock, Donald C. *The Complete Enochian Dictionary*. Samuel Weiser, Inc., York Beach, 1994.

McCoy, Edain. *Celtic Myth & Magick: Harness the Power of the Gods and Goddesses*. Llewellyn, St. Paul, 1997.

Wolf, Amber. *Elemental Power, Celtic Faerie Craft & Druidic Magic*. Llewellyn, St. Paul, 1997.

The use of the term "Eye of Newt" for the herb Lavender, is drawn from Silver RavenWolf's *Teen Witch Kit* book (pp 25, Llewellyn, St. Paul, 2000), and was pointed out to me by my ten-year-old daughter. I know of no other references that link these two together. Be that as it may, I have chosen to employ it in the recipes in this book.

About the Author

Parker J. Torrence was born in Denver, Colorado, in April of 1956, and spent his school years growing up in a small oilfield town in Wyoming. In 1974 he joined the U.S. Navy where he saw much of the Pacific Ocean, and spent 1995 on Diego Garcia (B.I.O.T.), before retiring in 1996.

It was while he was in the Navy and stationed on the USS Enterprise (1975-78) that he first discovered Wicca and the world of magick. The twenty-one years in the Navy following that discovery led him to explore many occult paths. Much of his career in the Navy he studied and worked as a solitary practitioner. In 1993, while taking a self-development seminar, he beheld a vision of the Goddess, and his path became more focused. It is that vision and that path which has lead him to the point from where this book was written.

On the Internet some people know him as St. Parker.

Parker, who calls himself a "simple" Pagan, currently lives near Midland, Texas, with his soul-mate, Wendy, their four children, two dogs, and a herd of seventeen cats.

To Contact the Author ::

The author always enjoys hearing from you, and can be contacted by email at sealandsky@eclecticmagick.com